# Alternate Routes

## An Alcohol Diversion Program

### YOUTH WORKBOOK

**Laura Burney Nissen, Ph.D., M.S.W.**

HAZELDEN®

Hazelden
Center City, Minnesota 55012-0176

1-800-328-9000
1-651-213-4590 (Fax)
www.hazelden.org

ISBN: 1-56838-874-8

Cover design by Theresa Gedig
Interior design by David Spohn
Typesetting by Tursso Companies

**About the Author**

Laura Burney Nissen, Ph.D., M.S.W., is currently an Associate Professor of Social Work at the Graduate School of Social Work, Portland State University. She is also Director of a national program for The Robert Wood Johnson Foundation entitled "Reclaiming Futures: Building Community Solutions to Substance Abuse and Delinquency." She lives in Portland, Oregon, with her husband, Don, and daughter, Hannah Grace.

**Hazelden Publishing and Educational Services** is a division of the Hazelden Foundation, a not-for-profit organization. Since 1949, Hazelden has been a leader in promoting the dignity and treatment of people afflicted with the disease of chemical dependency.

The mission of the foundation is to improve the quality of life for individuals, families, and communities by providing a national continuum of information, education, and recovery services that are widely accessible; to advance the field through research and training; and to improve our quality and effectiveness through continuous improvement and innovation.

Stemming from that, the mission of this division is to provide quality information and support to people wherever they may be in their personal journey—from education and early intervention, through treatment and recovery, to personal and spiritual growth.

Although our treatment programs do not necessarily use everything Hazelden publishes, our bibliotherapeutic materials support our mission and the Twelve Step philosophy upon which it is based. We encourage your comments and feedback.

The headquarters of the Hazelden Foundation are in Center City, Minnesota. Additional treatment facilities are located in Chicago, Illinois; New York, New York; Plymouth, Minnesota; St. Paul, Minnesota; and West Palm Beach, Florida. At these sites, we provide a continuum of care for men and women of all ages. Our Plymouth facility is designed specifically for youth and families.

For more information on Hazelden, please call **1-800-257-7800.** Or you may access our World Wide Web site on the Internet at **www.hazelden.org.**

Dedicated to the best in every youth. Show them what you've got.

# Contents

# Foreword

The fact that you find yourself in trouble for an alcohol offense is neither the end of the world nor something you should take lightly. Many young people experiment with alcohol even though it's against the law. Your use has caused you to be in trouble. Your reaction to finding yourself in this situation may be making it difficult for you to accept the consequences. You may feel that laws making it illegal for you to drink are unfair or that drinking ages should be changed. You may be upset about the circumstances of being caught or how the police treated you. Your parents' response may make this even more difficult for you.

Whatever you may think, the reality is alcohol can be a very big deal in your life—both now and later. Since alcohol has entered your life, this is a good time for you to give it some thought.

Thinking about alcohol might be something you believe you could do on your own. Perhaps you imagine spending a few minutes on it and that would be it. You could do that, but you most likely would be missing a lot. Learning about drinking—why you drink, how it might affect your friends and family, how it may affect your life and what you want your life to be—is complicated. It's like subjects in school— you learn much more taking a class and having a teacher than trying to teach yourself.

In my work I have seen many thousands of people and families who have been affected by drinking. Some cases are simple, like minors drinking. Most, however, are more serious. They are cases involving people injured or killed in accidents, careers lost, families destroyed, and crimes committed because of alcohol. Alcohol abuse is *the* single-largest contributor to the problems we have in our communities.

The tragedy of the problems created by alcohol is that it always cuts short the potential for people being healthy and happy.

You are at an age when you are beginning to paint a picture of what you want your life to look like. You are starting to see who you are, what you might be doing in a year or five years or twenty years, whether you want a family, what kind of career you might have. You have the potential to have the life you see. You can accomplish things that are now just dreams. You have before you the prospect that your life will be even better than you can imagine.

This workbook is designed to help you see this picture. To do this, you will be asked to think about who you are, what you want, how you're going to get there, and the skills and gifts that you have that can make this happen. And yes, it will ask you to think about your use of alcohol and how that plays into what you want your life to be. It will give you the chance to think about how your choices about alcohol mean more than you may have realized.

You cannot take back the choice you made to drink that brought you to this point. You can, however, be in control of the choices you make in the future. These choices can be good choices if you know who you are and what you want your life to be. You can make choices that will help you to your goal of being healthy, happy, and successful. Please take this opportunity to begin making mature decisions about the part alcohol will play in your life.

The Honorable Kip Leonard, Circuit Court Juvenile Judge
Lane County
Eugene, Oregon

# Introduction

Welcome to *Alternate Routes: An Alcohol Diversion Program.* This program is for you and other youth who have been referred to the courts because of an alcohol citation. You need to know several things as you open the *Alternate Routes* workbook and begin your work.

This workbook seeks to offer you a positive view of yourself. In this program, you'll think about your life and what you want out of it. No one can do this thinking for you, but there are people around you who can guide you. You will get as much out of this workbook as you put into it—so take a chance!

Alcohol has been identified as a risk in your life. This doesn't mean that you're an alcoholic or that anyone is trying to convince you that you are. But it does mean that adults in your life are worried about you and that some kind of behavior has gotten their attention. You may be frustrated with the amount of talking that you've been hearing lately—about you, your life, and your habits. Likely, a lot of adults have been giving you their opinions of your situation. In this program, you get to speak up for yourself and show the people around you that you have a plan to be successful and move on with your life.

If you do have a problem with alcohol, help is available. There's also a lot you can learn about how to help yourself. If you don't have a problem, you'll benefit from the chance to learn how to keep yourself safe for the future. If your drinking pattern has harmed anyone—even if you don't think you're an alcoholic—you can learn to make the situation right as you move through this program.

The *Alternate Routes* workbook can help you create a map to take you to your best self and the life you want. Crisis is opportunity. A situation involving alcohol has become a chance for you to learn about yourself, your life, and your direction. If you're willing, you will probably make new friends among others who are working on the same goals. Welcome to the opportunity to grow, change, and thrive.

Time to get started!

**Crisis ➡ Opportunity ➡ Motivation ➡ Self-knowledge, learning, and choice ➡ Success**

# Structure of the Curriculum: How It All Fits Together

This workbook contains twelve sections and a conclusion. Each section supports and challenges you to build a map for the future that fits your life.

| Title | What It's All About |
|---|---|
| 1. **Changes:** | What do you want to change in your life? |
| 2. **Identity:** | What are you all about? Who do you want to be? |
| 3. **Responsibility:** | Whom do you count on? Who counts on you? |
| 4. **How Alcohol Got You Here:** | What got you here and what can you do about it? |
| 5. **Relationships:** | To whom are you connected? Are you satisfied with your relationships? |
| 6. **Your Vision:** | What do you hope for most in your life? |
| 7. **Reaching:** | What positive risks do you need to take to get what you want in life? |
| 8. **Spirituality:** | What is your fuel for living? |
| 9. **Justice:** | What does fairness mean to you? What have you seen or experienced that is unfair? What can you do about unfairness? |
| 10. **Your Gifts:** | What is most special about you? |
| 11. **Having Fun:** | How do you let loose and relax? What are natural highs and how do you get them? |
| 12. **Staying Focused:** | What are your most important commitments? How do you keep on track? |
| **Conclusion—Your Plan for Success:** | What is your alternate route? |

**Each section contains three parts:**

1. *Questions to Ask Yourself*—Contains between fifteen and twenty questions to help you think about your ideas and feelings.

2. *Activities*—Contains ideas for things you can do to explore the questions further.

3. *Ideas for Your Plan for Success*—Contains points to remember as you lay out an alternate route, a route away from alcohol and other drugs.

# 1. Changes

## Overview

Everybody changes. You are changing all the time and so are your family, your friends, and the world around you. This section helps you think about change. You may think about it more than you ever have before. Do you feel like you can change your world, change your life, and change yourself? What changes have you made that you are proud of? What things have you not been able to change? Knowing how you change, when you change, and why you change is a source of power for a healthy and productive life.

### 1. Questions to Ask Yourself

a.  What is the biggest change you've ever experienced in your life?
    Was it good or bad?

    ..................................................................................................................

b.  What is an example of something about yourself that you changed
    for the worse? For the better? Did you know you were changing?
    Did you try to change? Now when you look back, what do you
    think about having gone through that change?

    ..................................................................................................................

c.  What is the biggest change you've ever seen in someone you care
    about? Were you involved in the change? Did you try to prevent the
    change from happening or did you help it to happen?

    ..................................................................................................................

d.   If people want to change their lives, what do they need to do? Try to think of three things.

.................................................................................................................................

e.   How have others tried to change your life? What do you think about the ways they've tried?

.................................................................................................................................

f.   What has been your biggest change in the last year? Was it a positive or negative change? Explain.

.................................................................................................................................

g.   Do you want to change anything about your life right now? What? Why?

.................................................................................................................................

h.   Is there anything changing in your life right now that you want to stay the same? What? Why?

.................................................................................................................................

i.   What are you like without alcohol? What are you like with it?

.................................................................................................................................

j.   What do you think of people who don't use alcohol and other drugs? Why do they choose not to use?

.................................................................................................................................

k.   Are there people in your life who have stopped using alcohol and other drugs? How did they do it?

.................................................................................................................................

## 2. Activities

a.  Changing is hard work, and it takes special skills. Draw a picture
    of a tool kit for change. What should be in it? Tell your group
    about something you've changed that makes you glad. What tools
    did you use?

b.  Draw a time line of your life. Divide it into three-year blocks
    (birth to age three, age four to age six, and so on). For each block
    of time, write what you consider to be the biggest changes you
    experienced.

c.  Extend the same time line ten years into the future. What changes
    do you think you will make in coming years? Write them on the
    time line.

d.  Interview family members or friends about the biggest change
    they've ever faced and how they handled it. What can you learn
    about yourself from their experiences?

    ................................................................................................................................

    ................................................................................................................................

    ................................................................................................................................

    ................................................................................................................................

e.  Draw a picture of one thing you'd like to change about yourself.

- You are changing all the time. You have the power to change in any way that you want. You also have the power to resist changes that feel uncomfortable or challenging. How are you using your power to change into the person you want to be?

  ............................................................................................................................

  ............................................................................................................................

- Sometime in your life, you accomplished something that you set your mind to do. What did this teach you? How can you use your knowledge and determination to set your life in positive motion?

  ............................................................................................................................

  ............................................................................................................................

  ............................................................................................................................

- Changing involves key steps—gathering information, getting support for making new choices, and practicing the new choices. Where can you get the ideas and help you need to stretch your life?

  ............................................................................................................................

  ............................................................................................................................

  ............................................................................................................................

- Realize that no one wants you to change *everything* about yourself. List something that is most likely to improve your life and the lives of those around you.

  ............................................................................................................................

  ............................................................................................................................

  ............................................................................................................................

*Sometime in your life you accomplished something that you set your mind to do.*

# 2. Identity

## Overview

Identity is about who you are—inside and outside. It is about your gender, your ethnicity/race, the family you come from, your religious/spiritual life, your culture(s), and much more. Because you are growing up, your identity is shifting from that of a child to that of a young adult. You are spreading your wings. The media send you a lot of messages about who you are and who you're supposed to become. Our society stereotypes youth in a variety of ways—often in ways that are very challenging. Your friends, your parents, and your community all play roles in helping you become the person that you are. This section helps you explore who you are and who you want to be.

### 1. Questions to Ask Yourself

a. What are the top five words you'd use to describe yourself? What one word describes the exact opposite of who you are?

    ...........................................................................................................................

b. How are you like other kids you know? How are you completely different from other kids you know?

    ...........................................................................................................................

c. How are you like members of your family? How are you completely unlike members of your family?

    ...........................................................................................................................

d. When people first meet you, what do you think they notice first? How do you feel about this? When people get to know you better, what do you think they notice? How do you feel about this?

.................................................................................................................................

e. What things do people know about you? What things don't people know about you . . . and might surprise them? How much have you trusted others with deeper parts of yourself?

.................................................................................................................................

f. What group of people makes you feel comfortable? Makes you feel uncomfortable? What does this say about who you are?

.................................................................................................................................

g. Have you ever found yourself or put yourself in a situation with people who are very different from you? What was it like? What did you learn?

.................................................................................................................................

h. Have people ever stereotyped or prejudged you? In what ways? What was that like? What did you learn from it? Have you ever stereotyped and prejudged others? How do you think this affected your relationship with that person or persons?

.................................................................................................................................

i. How do you think that the person you are will influence your choice of friends, spouse/partner, career, and lifestyle?

.................................................................................................................................

j. What famous or public person do you admire? What does this say about you? What famous or public person do you dislike? What does this say about you?

.................................................................................................................................

k.  Have you ever tried to hide your identity to please someone else? What was that like?

.........................................................................................

l.  How are you like people who live in your community? How are you unlike them? Do you ever feel that outsiders prejudge or stereotype your community? What effect do you think this has? Do you ever stereotype a community that is different from your own?

.........................................................................................

m.  What role does religion/spirituality play in your life? What messages about your place in the world come from your experiences in this area?

.........................................................................................

n.  How has alcohol impacted your vision of yourself?

.........................................................................................

## 2. Activities

a.  Make a collage that describes you. Find magazine pictures or make drawings that illustrate the five words you used to describe yourself in question a. Paste them on a large sheet of paper. You might lie on a long piece of butcher paper and have a friend draw an outline of your body. Then paste your pictures inside the outline to make a life-size collage.

b.  Go somewhere specifically to be surrounded by people who are different from you in manner, custom, and, if possible, language. This might be an ethnic festival, a worship service, or another community event that involves people or activities that are new to you. Make sure the situation is safe before you go. Jot down some thoughts about what you observe, and what you learn about yourself in that situation.

*How are you like people who live in your community?*

*How are you unlike them?*

c. Interview ten people who know you well. Ask them a few questions about their impressions of you. Compare their answers. What patterns do you see?

d. Make a collage of yourself as a house—with various parts of your life and your identity showing up as different rooms. What would the rooms be? What would be in them? What would the rooms and furnishings symbolize?

## 3. Ideas for Your Plan for Success

- You may need help to become acquainted with new parts of yourself. Knowing oneself is a lifelong process full of mystery and twists and turns. But the more you know, the more successful you'll be.

- Everyone has things they like and dislike about themselves. Celebrate the terrific parts of you and acknowledge that you have some work to do to make yourself a better person. How has alcohol impacted your vision of yourself?

  .......................................................................................................................

  .......................................................................................................................

  .......................................................................................................................

- Do you know the very best parts of yourself? What are they? Are you showing these to the world?

  .......................................................................................................................

  .......................................................................................................................

  .......................................................................................................................

# 3. Responsibility

## Overview

Simply put, responsibility is about who is counting on you—in your family and friendships, in your community, and even in your nation. Responsibility is about living up to your commitments—and being accountable if you break those commitments. This section focuses on the issue of responsibility in your life and helps you understand the relationship of responsibility to your own well-being and the well-being of those around you.

### 1. Questions to Ask Yourself

a.  What are your most important commitments in life? To whom did you make them? Where did they come from? Who counts on you? What for?

    .................................................................................................

b.  Give an example of a time when someone didn't follow through on a commitment to you. What effect did this have on your life?

    .................................................................................................

c.  How does your involvement in this program relate to a broken commitment? How can you best demonstrate responsibility during this program and through the coming months?

    .................................................................................................

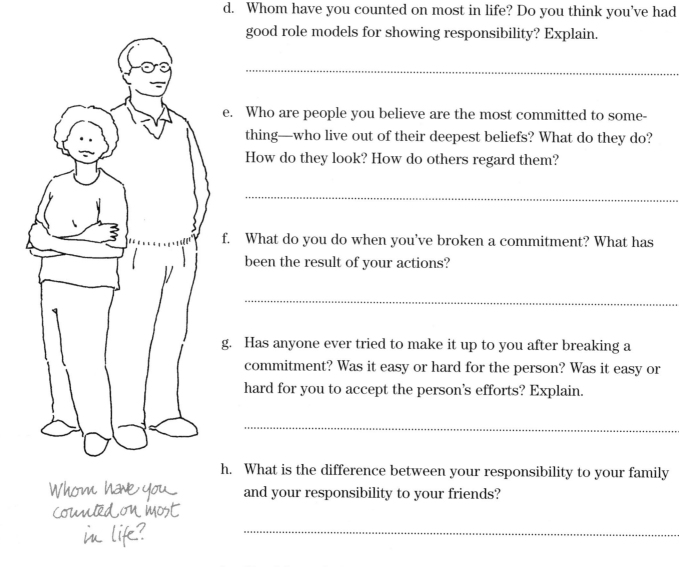

d.  Whom have you counted on most in life? Do you think you've had good role models for showing responsibility? Explain.

.......................................................................................................................

e.  Who are people you believe are the most committed to something—who live out of their deepest beliefs? What do they do? How do they look? How do others regard them?

.......................................................................................................................

f.  What do you do when you've broken a commitment? What has been the result of your actions?

.......................................................................................................................

g.  Has anyone ever tried to make it up to you after breaking a commitment? Was it easy or hard for the person? Was it easy or hard for you to accept the person's efforts? Explain.

.......................................................................................................................

h.  What is the difference between your responsibility to your family and your responsibility to your friends?

.......................................................................................................................

i.  Should people be responsible to their communities? What does responsibility to one's community mean to you? What examples have you seen?

.......................................................................................................................

j.  What does personal responsibility mean? What does commitment to yourself mean? What are examples of both?

.......................................................................................................................

Whom have you counted on most in life?

Do you think you've had good role models for showing responsibility?

k.  Give an example of a commitment that you have chosen and one that was given to you without your consent. How are they alike and different?

    .......................................................................................................................................

a.  List ten commitments that you have kept, and ten that you have not kept. Talk to your group about your feelings regarding what you see on either list. Talk about which of the broken commitments you might be able to make right in some way. Who would be most proud of you for doing so?

    ...........................................          ...........................................

    ...........................................          ...........................................

    ...........................................          ...........................................

    ...........................................          ...........................................

    ...........................................          ...........................................

b.  Explore ways to make your commitment to your community come to life. Learn about opportunities to volunteer in your community in creative ways and then choose one activity in which to participate. Write a short report of your experience.

    .......................................................................................................................................

    .......................................................................................................................................

    .......................................................................................................................................

    .......................................................................................................................................

    .......................................................................................................................................

    .......................................................................................................................................

    .......................................................................................................................................

Responsibility

c. Draw a comic strip showing yourself making amends for a commitment that you have broken. What steps will you take to move toward making things right? What will the final scene be like?

d. Pick a situation in your life right now that involves a commitment. Go out of your way to fulfill the commitment in a positive manner. Talk to your group about the experience in detail. How did it feel to surprise someone by doing more than was expected?

........................................................................................................................................

........................................................................................................................................

........................................................................................................................................

e. Draw a picture comparing two commitments you've made to yourself—one which you've kept and one which you've not kept so far. Write the feelings you notice on your drawing.

## 3. Ideas for Your Plan for Success

- How you fulfill commitments is an important part of your experiences with this program. Can people count on you? Can you count on yourself? In what ways?

  ........................................................................................................................

  ........................................................................................................................

  ........................................................................................................................

- To be successful in life, you must focus on your commitments. What are your most important commitments to yourself, your family, your friends, and your community? How can you demonstrate this commitment every day?

  ........................................................................................................................

  ........................................................................................................................

  ........................................................................................................................

  ........................................................................................................................

- Can you maintain a commitment to not drink while you're in this program? If you can't, do you need a deeper level of help, support, or treatment? If you continue to drink, who is most likely to be hurt by your decision?

  ........................................................................................................................

  ........................................................................................................................

  ........................................................................................................................

  ........................................................................................................................

Responsibility

# 4. How Alcohol Got You Here

## Overview

Perhaps you're wondering if you might be headed for trouble. The bottom line is that alcohol has brought you to this program. Perhaps your situation was an accident, a one-time incident, or a lapse of good judgment. Or maybe your behavior has been steadily getting more dangerous. You might be drinking a little more than you meant to, doing things you're not proud of when drinking, or forgetting what you've done when you were drinking.

Whatever the reason, looking for signs of trouble and potential danger for yourself and other people is a smart thing to do. The hard work you're doing in this program will open your eyes to the facts and prepare you to meet your goals in life.

### 1. Questions to Ask Yourself

a. How do you feel about the fact that you're sitting in an alcohol diversion program? Who is most concerned about you?

.........................................................................................

b. What behaviors have caused others to express concern about you?

.........................................................................................

c. Why do people drink? How do they know if they have a problem?

.........................................................................................

*How do you feel about the fact that you're sitting in an alcohol diversion program?*

d.   Have you ever seen or done anything you wish you hadn't while drinking? List an example or two.

.......................................................................................................................

e.   Have you ever blacked out during a drinking session? Do you ever get hangovers?

.......................................................................................................................

f.   Have you ever failed to meet any commitments because of drinking? Explain.

.......................................................................................................................

g.   What risks to others and yourself do you take when drinking?

.......................................................................................................................

h.   What have you missed out on because of your drinking?

.......................................................................................................................

i.   When others are drinking, are you able to abstain (keep from drinking)?

.......................................................................................................................

j.   Do you ever have fun without drinking or being in drinking situations? When?

.......................................................................................................................

k.   How does the drinking of close family members or friends impact your life?

.......................................................................................................................

## 2. Activities

a. Participate in an alcohol awareness session in a group setting. (Note: Be sure to read any handouts provided about the effects of drinking on the human body.)

b. Visit people who have been harmed by drunk drivers. Discuss what you've heard with someone you trust.

c. Find out what goes on in alcohol treatment programs, and what to do if you or someone you care about needs to get into one.

d. Find out what kinds of alcohol-prevention activities are going on in your school, place of worship, or community. Challenge yourself to support efforts to get youth to delay their first use of alcohol as long as possible.

## 3. Ideas for Your Plan for Success

- Your thoughts on the ways that alcohol brought you here are personal. No one knows what you're thinking or feeling unless you tell them. Write your own "statement of accountability" and share it with someone you trust. A statement of accountability shows that you take responsibility for your actions.

..............................................................................................................................

..............................................................................................................................

..............................................................................................................................

- Think about the people who are most likely to notice changes in your drinking behaviors and patterns. What changes will they see?

..............................................................................................................................

..............................................................................................................................

..............................................................................................................................

How Alcohol Got You Here

# 5. Relationships

## Overview

Even if you like to be alone, the truth is that none of us gets along all by ourselves. Relationships are a part of everyone's life. Everyone has a variety of relationships—close, casual, healthy, strained, easy, and difficult. You probably have all of these types and more. To be happy, healthy, and successful, you need to know which relationships you can count on. The best ones are those in which people are mutually committed to each other's happiness and well-being, but much can be learned from relationships with people we don't like or don't get along with.

Through relationships, we help each other grow and have fun, comfort each other through hard times, teach each other valuable lessons, and experience all that life has to offer. What are your relationships like? As a family member or friend—what are you like to be in a relationship with?

This section helps you think about your relationships and how you can improve them.

### 1. Questions to Ask Yourself

a. What are the most important relationships in your life? Why? What is the best thing about them?

.........................................................................................................

b. What is the biggest difference between your relationships with your family and your relationships with your friends?

.........................................................................................................

c. Whom do you count on most in life? What shows you that you can count on them?

..................................................................................................................................................

d. Who counts on you? What shows them that they can count on you?

..................................................................................................................................................

e. Have you ever ended a relationship? Why? Give an example of something that would make you end a relationship.

..................................................................................................................................................

f. How do you start new relationships? Do you like making new friends? Is making friends easy or difficult for you?

..................................................................................................................................................

g. When you are at your best in relationships, what is it like? What are you doing? What are others doing? What is easy and what is difficult about your closest relationships?

..................................................................................................................................................

*Whom do you count on most in life?*

*What shows you that you can count on them?*

h. What advice do you have for people who want to get to know you?

..................................................................................................................................................

i. Whom do you love? What are different kinds of love? Who have been your biggest teachers about love?

..................................................................................................................................................

j. How does use of alcohol affect your relationships? Have you ever lost a relationship because of drinking? Have you ever been hurt because of alcohol (or other drugs)?

..................................................................................................................................................

k. What is support? Do you have enough support in your life? How can you get more? Do you give support to others? Do you give enough support or too much? Why?

..................................................................................................................

l. Has your drinking caused pain or injury to another person? What does accountability in relationships mean? What can you do to show accountability for any harm your actions may have caused?

..................................................................................................................

## 2. Activities

a. Imagine that alcohol is a person. Write a letter to Alcohol about your relationship with it. What would you say?

..................................................................................................................

..................................................................................................................

..................................................................................................................

..................................................................................................................

..................................................................................................................

..................................................................................................................

..................................................................................................................

..................................................................................................................

..................................................................................................................

b. Write five letters to people who have loved and supported you. Thank them for their relationship. Send the letters if it feels safe to do so.

c.  Complete the following:

| Five things I can do to improve my relationship with myself: | Five things I can do to improve my relationship with my family: | Five things I can do to improve my relationship with my friends: |
| --- | --- | --- |
|  |  |  |

d.  Write a letter to your community (however you define it). Talk about the kind of citizen you've been, what you'd like to do more and less of, and how you feel about living there. Discuss your ideas for making your community a better place for youth and what you will do to help. Talk to your group facilitator about the possibility of sending your letter.

### 3. Ideas for Your Plan for Success

- The relationships that support and encourage you to be the best that you can be are your most powerful resource. Make sure that you know who these people are in your everyday life.

- If you aren't satisfied with the quality of your relationships, know that you can do a lot to improve them. You can also build new relationships that will be better for you. Remember, too, just because you make new friends, doesn't mean you have to stop caring for old ones.

# 6. Your Vision

## Overview

This section is about your aspirations. Aspirations are things that you hope for, dream about, or wish for in your life and in the lives of those you care about. Some people believe that our aspirations ultimately determine the course of our lives, no matter what troubles we may have. Do you have a vision of the life you want? If so, what are you doing to make your vision come true? If you don't have a vision, are you willing to think about the idea that a better life, a happier and more fulfilling life, may be just around the corner? Take a chance. Use this section to take your vision out for a walk. What does it have to teach you?

### 1. Questions to Ask Yourself

a. Do you ever set goals? What are some examples? Are they mostly short term (next month or year) or longer term (more than a year)?

..................................................................................................

b. What is your vision of the life you want? Have you ever told anyone about it?

..................................................................................................

c. What are your hopes for the kind of family life you'll have in ten years? Job or career? Friends?

..................................................................................................

d.  What does success in life mean to you? Who are the most successful people you know?

.........................................................................................................................................

e.  If you won a million dollars in the lottery, what would you *really do* with the money?

.........................................................................................................................................

f.  If you could change something big about the problems in the world, what would you change and why? How would you do it?

.........................................................................................................................................

g.  Name five different careers that you would like to explore. What resources exist in your school and community to help you explore them?

.........................................................................................................................................

.........................................................................................................................................

.........................................................................................................................................

.........................................................................................................................................

.........................................................................................................................................

h.  As you look over your list of careers, are there any that you think are out of reach? Why? Who in your life has made you feel this way?

.........................................................................................................................................

i.  Imagine that you are mentoring a child who has no vision of a better life. How would you help him or her find a vision and then move toward making it a reality?

.........................................................................................................................................

a.  Imagine your best vision about your life in ten years. What kind of family and career will you have? What did you have to overcome to achieve your goals? Share your vision with someone in your group and then listen to his or her vision. Write an encouraging letter to each other about achieving dreams.

........................................................................................................

........................................................................................................

........................................................................................................

........................................................................................................

........................................................................................................

........................................................................................................

........................................................................................................

........................................................................................................

........................................................................................................

b.  Take your list of careers to your school counselor or other trusted adult. Ask for help in finding adults to interview about these careers. During the interview, find out how the person achieved his or her career goals and how you might enter that field.

*Imagine your best vision about your life in ten years.*

c.  Make a map to show how you'll reach your vision of success. Draw a picture of yourself on the far left side of a sheet of paper (or use a photo). Draw a picture of your vision on the far right side. In between draw the challenges you will likely encounter on the way to your vision. Show tools or skills you'll need to overcome these challenges. Then draw a strong line connecting where you are to where you want to be. Hang your map in a place where you'll see it regularly.

*What kind of family and career will you have?*

Your Vision

d.  Ask people you care about and trust what their visions in life are.
    Do they feel they can achieve these visions? Why or why not?
    Listen carefully.

    ................................................................................................................

    ................................................................................................................

    ................................................................................................................

e.  Start a journal using an inexpensive notebook. A journal is a
    private place where you can keep track of your thoughts. Write
    down your ideas about things you'd like to do in your life. Include
    examples of people you know who are working toward or who
    have achieved these things. How are they doing it? Write down
    song lyrics that speak to the power of having a vision of success
    in life.

### 3. Ideas for Your Plan for Success

*   Think about a vision in life as fuel to power your success. A vision
    can also be a tool to help you decide what is important and what is
    not. What are your visions? Has anyone ever made you feel as if
    you can't achieve these things?

    ................................................................................................................

    ................................................................................................................

    ................................................................................................................

*   What things do you now do that will help you achieve your vision
    of success? What behaviors are likely to interfere with your vision?
    Get as honest as you can about this.

    ................................................................................................................

    ................................................................................................................

    ................................................................................................................

# 7. Reaching

## Overview

Risk is part of life. Maybe you like taking risks that give you a rush. You take chances in ways that make you feel alive and free and in the moment. This section is about a bigger kind of risk. It is about reaching into new experiences of life such as trying a new behavior, making new friends, starting a new job or class, or taking advantage of an opportunity. This type of risk may cause discomfort or anxiety because you don't always know how things will turn out.

Most people don't take many risks with their behavior. They get into a "comfort zone" where they do the same thing over and over. Even when they are frustrated, tired, or just want to give up, they have a hard time getting out of that rut. To get the life you want, you need to grow and change. You must learn how to REACH out in new ways to new people and take a chance now and then. Part of having the life you want is learning how to create a vision for yourself. Almost as important is developing the ability to reach toward your vision and get what you want.

### 1. Questions to Ask Yourself

a. What is the biggest risk you've ever taken? Was it a positive risk or a dangerous risk? Explain.

......................................................................................................

b. What is courage? Do you think you are courageous? When is it smart to be brave and when is it better to be cautious?

......................................................................................................

c.  Have you ever taken a chance on someone or something that turned out badly? What was it like?

.................................................................................................................

.................................................................................................................

d.  Think about having a vision in your life. Then think of people you know who are living their visions. What risks did they take along the path to their visions? How did they show courage?

.................................................................................................................

.................................................................................................................

e.  Has it been a positive risk to come to this program, meet new people, and change your behaviors? Describe your feelings.

.................................................................................................................

.................................................................................................................

f.  List three new experiences you'd like to have that you believe would make you a better person. What would be involved in trying them?

.................................................................................................................

.................................................................................................................

.................................................................................................................

g.  How would you counsel someone who wants your advice about a big risk he or she is about to take? What would you say to help the person consider all the options and make a good decision?

.................................................................................................................

.................................................................................................................

a. Share your list of new experiences with your group or a trusted friend. Ask to listen to their lists. Talk about and compare the different risks that people are willing to experience. Why do you think different things are risky for different people?

........................................................................................................................

........................................................................................................................

........................................................................................................................

........................................................................................................................

b. Try to do at least one experience from your list. Get a positive person in your life to join you. Share the outcome with your group.

c. Read a book about or interview someone you consider to be a great or successful person. Look for the risks that he or she took on the way to success.

## 3. Ideas for Your Plan for Success

• Know your style of taking chances. Are you willing to risk feeling uncomfortable to try something new if you think it might make your life better?

........................................................................................................................

• Know that many things worth having in life are worth taking a chance on. Be sure that you think through all of your options before taking a chance. If you decide that the risk is worthwhile, that neither you nor anyone else will be harmed, and that it has the potential to make your life better—go for it and good luck.

Reaching

- Remember that your use of alcohol most likely has impacted the kinds of chances you've taken. People take crazy risks when they are drinking. Think about ways to have fun that don't include that kind of risk taking as you proceed with your plan for success.

.......................................................................................................

.......................................................................................................

.......................................................................................................

.......................................................................................................

People take crazy risks when they are drinking.

Think about ways to have fun that don't include that kind of risk taking as you proceed with your plan for success.

# 8. Spirituality

## Overview

Spirituality is the personal fuel that you use to get through your life. What do you believe about spirituality? About right and wrong? About where you come from before you're born, and where you go when you die? All of these questions and many more are contained within a world of different religions and spiritual practices. Your family background may have provided you with a strong religious base, or you may have had less formal, but still very spiritual, experiences. You also may never have explored these parts of life before. This section focuses on the role of spirituality in your life and helps you think about the ways in which your spiritual life might relate to your health and success in daily life. Every religious and spiritual path is valuable. As you learn about your own spiritual path, remember that you can also learn from others who have a different, but nonetheless valuable, path from your own.

### 1. Questions to Ask Yourself

a. Do you believe in a Power greater than yourself? How did you come to have this belief?

   ............................................................................................................

b. Who are people you consider to be spiritual? What are they like? What do they do?

   ............................................................................................................

c.  What is the most spiritual experience you've ever had? Was anyone else involved or were you alone?

......................................................................................................................

d.  Do you ever do things that make you feel spiritual? What are they? Do you do them often? What are places you have been that you consider spiritual? Do you go to these places often?

......................................................................................................................

e.  Why do you believe people are put on earth?

......................................................................................................................

f.  What difference do you wish to make in the world? How will the world be different (and better) because you were here?

......................................................................................................................

g.  How do people grow in their spiritual lives? Who are people you would trust as spiritual leaders?

......................................................................................................................

h.  What does right and wrong mean to you? Where did you learn about right and wrong? Has this changed over time for you?

......................................................................................................................

i.  Do you believe people are basically good or bad? Explain.

......................................................................................................................

j.  Have you ever apologized to anyone for hurting him or her?

......................................................................................................................

k.  Have you ever forgiven anyone? Have you ever been forgiven for something you've done that hurt someone?

......................................................................................................................

*Do you ever do things that make you feel spiritual?*

*What are they?*

l.  What are you most grateful for?

........................................................................................................................

a.  Imagine that your past year has been a spiritual quest. Draw a
    picture about a spiritual lesson that you learned.

b.  List one hundred things that you are grateful for. Push yourself and
    keep going even if you get stuck. Most people have MUCH more to
    be grateful for than they normally think about.

........................................................................................................................

........................................................................................................................

........................................................................................................................

........................................................................................................................

........................................................................................................................

........................................................................................................................

........................................................................................................................

........................................................................................................................

........................................................................................................................

........................................................................................................................

Spirituality

c.  Visit a place you consider spiritual. Write a poem about what you
    see, hear, smell, and feel in that place.

    ........................................................................................................

    ........................................................................................................

    ........................................................................................................

    ........................................................................................................

d.  Write your "spiritual autobiography" in a few pages. What is the
    story of your spiritual life and growth since you were little up until
    now? Start by jotting down some thoughts below.

    ........................................................................................................

    ........................................................................................................

    ........................................................................................................

    ........................................................................................................

    ........................................................................................................

e.  Draw a picture showing the relationship of your spiritual self and
    your use of alcohol.

- Think about your spiritual fuel for living. Note the degree to which it is part of your life. Has it been developing for some time, or is it pretty new?

..................................................................................................................

..................................................................................................................

..................................................................................................................

..................................................................................................................

- Your spirituality might relate to your success. Is it a resource you have looked at in a serious way? Explain.

..................................................................................................................

..................................................................................................................

..................................................................................................................

..................................................................................................................

- Think about the potential that alcohol and other drugs have to interfere with your spiritual well-being. Write your thoughts below.

..................................................................................................................

..................................................................................................................

..................................................................................................................

..................................................................................................................

# 9. Justice

## Overview

We live in a world that is full of conflict and unfairness. When you watch the evening news, or talk to people in your community, or study history, it is easy to see many examples of things that are not right or just. Perhaps you have experienced unfairness in your life—either as a victim or as someone who was unfair to others. Almost everyone has experiences in both places. You may be frustrated by the lack of fairness and justice in the world. This section invites you to think about right and wrong as you see them happening in the world around you. It asks what you believe you can do to increase the chances that justice will prevail.

### 1. Questions to Ask Yourself

a.  What should communities provide to encourage youth to grow up healthy and positive? Do you think your community provides these things? Why? Why not? Is there anything you can do to improve the situation? Explain.

    ............................................................................................................

b.  When you look at the world around you, what do you like most and what makes you angry? Why?

    ............................................................................................................

c.  Have you ever done anything on purpose to make the world a better place? What was it? What was it like? Who was involved?

..................................................................................................................................

d.  Do you think life is fair? Have you ever been treated unfairly? How did it make you feel?

..................................................................................................................................

e.  How do people behave when they are treated in an unjust manner? Have you seen this in your life?

..................................................................................................................................

f.  Do you believe people have a responsibility to make the world a better place? If so, where did you learn this?

..................................................................................................................................

*Do you believe you are a positive force in your community?*

g.  Do you believe you are a positive force in your community? What do you do that shows positive behavior to those close to you? What do you do that shows positive behavior to people who don't know you?

..................................................................................................................................

h.  If people have harmed others, what should they do to right that wrong? Have you ever righted a wrong you caused? What was the wrong? What did you do to make things right?

..................................................................................................................................

i.  Is there anything about your drinking (or the drinking behaviors of friends or peers) that has caused or has the potential to cause harm in your community? What are your ideas about how to deal with this?

..................................................................................................................................

## 2. Activities

a.  List twenty things you could do to make life better for others in
    your neighborhood.

........................................          ........................................

........................................          ........................................

........................................          ........................................

........................................          ........................................

........................................          ........................................

........................................          ........................................

........................................          ........................................

........................................          ........................................

........................................          ........................................

........................................          ........................................

b.  Share your list of twenty things to do with two other people. Ask
    what they think of the ideas on your list. Act on at least one of
    your ideas in the next two weeks.

c.  Write a letter to a community leader about the adequacy of youth
    services and programs in your neighborhood.

d.  Visit parents who have lost children in drunk driving accidents.
    Talk to another person about what you heard, saw, and felt during
    your visit.

e.  Write a letter to the person who referred you to this program (you
    may or may not send the letter later). Talk about what you've
    learned and how you plan to become a more positive force in your
    community.

f. Now, imagine you're actually talking to the judge who referred you to this program. Describe the behaviors that demonstrate that you are a positive force in your community. Role-play this with your group.

.......................................................................................................................................

.......................................................................................................................................

.......................................................................................................................................

g. Visit a homeless shelter or other community service program for youth. Ask to volunteer for a day. Tell another person what you learned.

## 3. Ideas for Your Plan for Success

- Most communities suffer from injustice and unfairness in a variety of ways. You have the power to make your community a better place. Think about how you will use that power.

.......................................................................................................................................

.......................................................................................................................................

- Think about how your behaviors (especially drinking) have influenced the well-being of those around you. Have you ever hurt or risked hurting anyone with your drinking?

.......................................................................................................................................

.......................................................................................................................................

- Your experience with this program can make you a leader in talking to other youth who struggle with substance use in their lives. Think about how you'll use that leadership in positive ways.

.......................................................................................................................................

.......................................................................................................................................

# 10. Your Gifts

## Overview

There will never be another you. Although you have problems, frustrations, and challenges, you are also unique, special, and precious. You have the potential to bring gifts and positive momentum to those around you every day. Do you know what your gifts are? Do you use them and share them with the world around you? This section invites you to think about your valuable gifts and how you make those gifts part of your life and the lives of others.

### 1. Questions to Ask Yourself

a.  What do you think is most special about you?

   ...................................................................................................

b.  What special skills or talents do you have? What do you do well? Who knows this about you (close friends, family)?

   ...................................................................................................

c.  Describe something you did for which you are very proud. What was it, how did it happen, and who was involved?

   ...................................................................................................

d.  What is special about your family members? What is an example of something they do well?

   ...................................................................................................

e.  Describe a time when you handled a difficult situation well. What happened and who was involved?

    ...........................................................................................................................................

f.  Describe a time when you made someone feel better. What happened and who was involved?

    ...........................................................................................................................................

g.  What would you never want to change about yourself? Why?

    ...........................................................................................................................................

h.  What is the strongest thing about you? Why? How do you know this?

    ...........................................................................................................................................

i.  When you are at your best, what is that like and what are you doing? Who is around you?

    ...........................................................................................................................................

j.  What would your family members say they value most about you?

    ...........................................................................................................................................

k.  What would your friends say they value most about you?

    ...........................................................................................................................................

l.  What would people in your community say they value most about you?

    ...........................................................................................................................................

m. Describe something you should have won an award for.

    ...........................................................................................................................................

n.  Name a gift you have that no one or few people know about, but that you'd like to develop.

...............................................................................................................

o.  Does alcohol interfere with your special skills or talents? Explain.

...............................................................................................................

## 2. Activities

a.  List twenty things you like about yourself. Start them all with the phrase "You are . . ." Have someone you trust read them to you. Have that person make a list for himself or herself and then read it back to him or her.

| | |
|---|---|
| .......................................... | .......................................... |
| .......................................... | .......................................... |
| .......................................... | .......................................... |
| .......................................... | .......................................... |
| .......................................... | .......................................... |
| .......................................... | .......................................... |
| .......................................... | .......................................... |
| .......................................... | .......................................... |
| .......................................... | .......................................... |
| .......................................... | .......................................... |

b.  Make a collage that shows the many gifts that you have. Put the collage in a place where you will see it regularly.

c.  Write a statement called "Why the World Is a Better Place Because I Am Here." Share it with someone you trust.

.........................................................................................................................................

.........................................................................................................................................

.........................................................................................................................................

d.  Share your gifts by helping someone in your group develop a skill or talent. In turn, ask someone to help you develop a strength.

### 3. Ideas for Your Plan for Success

- Your gifts are precious—just like you. There will never be another you. Be sure to value your strengths and your abilities.

- Don't forget that while we can't always solve every problem, we can almost always get stronger. Let your strengths provide you with energy and hope during times of stress and trouble.

*Your gifts are precious—just like you. There will never be another you. Be sure to value your strengths and abilities.*

# 11. Having Fun

## Overview

Having fun—enjoying friends, family, the world around you—is a big part of life. Healthy, happy, and positive people have a wide range of ways for having fun and enjoying life. They know how to balance work and play. They also know how to balance having fun with staying safe and healthy. Some things are fun, but they aren't necessarily safe. This section helps you explore ways of having fun and seeking the "natural highs" essential to a good life. How much fun are you having?

### 1. Questions to Ask Yourself

a.  How do you like to have fun? Do you have fun a lot?

    .................................................................................................................

b.  Do you think you're fun to be around? Do you think you're more fun when you're drinking? Have you ever felt fun when not drinking?

    .................................................................................................................

c.  Who are people in your life who are really fun? Can you think of people who have fun without drinking, or are the people who come to mind drinkers? What does your answer say about you?

    .................................................................................................................

d. List fifty things you like to do to have fun that don't involve drinking. Push yourself. The more ways people have to relax and enjoy life, the healthier they are. What is on your list?

..............................................................................................................

..............................................................................................................

..............................................................................................................

..............................................................................................................

..............................................................................................................

..............................................................................................................

..............................................................................................................

..............................................................................................................

..............................................................................................................

..............................................................................................................

..............................................................................................................

..............................................................................................................

..............................................................................................................

e. Which of the fifty things can you do for little or no cost?

..............................................................................................................

..............................................................................................................

..............................................................................................................

..............................................................................................................

..............................................................................................................

f.  What makes you laugh?

.................................................................................................................

.................................................................................................................

.................................................................................................................

.................................................................................................................

g.  What is the most fun you've ever had? What were you doing? Who
    was involved?

.................................................................................................................

.................................................................................................................

.................................................................................................................

.................................................................................................................

h.  What is the most fun you've ever had with your family? Was it
    recently or a long time ago?

.................................................................................................................

.................................................................................................................

.................................................................................................................

.................................................................................................................

i.  Can you have fun alone or do you prefer to be in a group?

.................................................................................................................

j.  What new way of having fun would you like to explore?

.................................................................................................................

.................................................................................................................

.................................................................................................................

Having Fun

k.  What is not fun in your life? Can you do anything to make it more enjoyable? Explain.

......................................................................................................................

......................................................................................................................

......................................................................................................................

l.  Think back over the last two months. Have you had fun without drinking? If not, what does this tell you about yourself?

......................................................................................................................

......................................................................................................................

......................................................................................................................

## 2. Activities

a.  Visit with successful people whom you admire. Ask how they balance work and fun in their lives.

b.  Do something fun every day that is good for you and those around you. Jot down on a calendar what you do.

c.  Share your list of fifty fun things to do with your group. Based on what others in your group say, add ten new activities you'd like to try.

..................................................    ..................................................

..................................................    ..................................................

..................................................    ..................................................

..................................................    ..................................................

..................................................    ..................................................

- Having fun is an important part of life. The point is to not stop having fun by examining your behavior. Instead, the point is to learn about and try out a wider range of ways for having fun that are good for you and those around you.

- No one can argue that drinking can cause people to feel temporarily good, silly, and positive. The problem is that drinking carries with it other dangers and risks. Adults are free to choose to drink responsibly. As a youth, the law says that you do not have this freedom. Only you can commit to finding ways to have fun that keep you healthy and moving toward your goals in life. Drinking is not the answer. Strengthen your range of ways to have fun and then go for it!

*Strengthen your range of ways to have fun and then go for it!*

Having Fun

# 12. Staying Focused

## Overview

Frustrations, detours—things that get in your way and keep you from your goals—are part of life. Successful and happy people don't necessarily have fewer setbacks. They have simply learned how to cope with them effectively and not lose their focus. This section asks you to think about the way you deal with setbacks and frustrations. Do you get angry or sad? Do you give up or lash out? Do you hurt yourself when things don't go your way? Do you expect to have your plans derailed? How do you learn to stick with a plan once you have worked so hard to develop it—no matter what happens? Perseverance means hanging in there despite all the odds and never losing track of the goal. In this section, you'll decide if you're satisfied with your ability to persevere.

   If you've made it this far into the workbook, you've done a huge amount of work getting to know yourself and what makes you tick. You've done a lot of searching and thinking and reflecting and working! Now it's time to take all of that information and begin connecting it to a plan of action. When you started this program, you did so because a problem had been identified. By now you realize that a problem is more than a hassle—it is also an opportunity. If you've stuck with the program, you realize that the problem you came in with has given you the chance to learn about yourself and others in a whole new way. You are almost ready to fulfill your commitment to the program and celebrate its completion. This section looks at endings as new beginnings. It helps you look at your current commitments and move into a plan for success that will take you beyond this program and into the rest of your life.

a. How do you know when you're frustrated with something you're working on? How do those around you know? Give an example of a time when you've been frustrated. What makes you angry? What do you do when you're angry?

......................................................................................................................................

b. How do you get yourself back on track when you've had a set-back? Give an example of a time you did this.

......................................................................................................................................

c. Whom can you turn to when you're about to give up? Who would be most disappointed if you didn't do the right thing for you?

......................................................................................................................................

d. What makes you sad? What do you do when you get sad? How do people around you know that you're sad? Do you have someone you could talk to if you get depressed?

......................................................................................................................................

e. Give an example of something you accomplished that was really difficult and took a long time. How did you do it?

......................................................................................................................................

f. Who are the caring adults in your life who are encouraging you to grow? Do you appreciate their efforts? Do you appreciate some efforts more than others? What do you appreciate and why?

......................................................................................................................................

g. What are three goals you have for the next week? For the next month? For the next year? Does anyone else know about your goals?

......................................................................................................................................

h.  Do you use a calendar or planner to keep yourself organized? If not, would you be willing to try?

......................................................................................................................................................

i.  Who are people who would be willing to support you in getting to your goals? What kind of regular contact could you have with them to check in?

......................................................................................................................................................

j.  Have you let any goals fall away recently or become distracted from working on them? Did alcohol (either drinking it or recovering from partying) interfere in any way with progress you had planned to make on your goals?

......................................................................................................................................................

k.  Have you ever helped anyone you cared about work toward one of his or her goals? How did it feel?

......................................................................................................................................................

l.  Do you have any fears about asking people to support you? What are they? Have you ever asked people to support you before?

......................................................................................................................................................

m.  Balance is an important part of resiliency (the ability to bounce back). How is your physical balance? Do you eat in healthy ways? Get enough exercise and rest? Balance work and play?

......................................................................................................................................................

## 2. Activities

a.  Make a large calendar for the next month. Write down a couple of goals you have for the month. Fill in your commitments for each day, but remember to have some fun every day too!

b. Look through your answers in this workbook. Make a poster of the biggest distractions you face in meeting your goals. Write strong words of encouragement on your poster. Show how you'll overcome the distractions.

c. Identify three people in your life whom you trust. Ask them to promise to tell you if they see you getting off track. Commit yourself to honoring them by listening if they do give you feedback.

.............................................................................................................................

.............................................................................................................................

d. Fill out and share the following "balance sheet." For each area of your life, give examples of ways you feel balance and satisfaction and ways you feel stress and potential difficulty. Share your balance sheet with someone you trust.

|  | Ways I'm in Balance | Ways I'm Out of Balance |
|---|---|---|
| Personal/Physical |  |  |
| Relationships *(family and friends)* |  |  |
| School/Work |  |  |
| Free Time/Fun |  |  |

- Anybody can make a promise or a plan. Keeping it is much more difficult. After doing so much work in this workbook, you have power you didn't have before to help you achieve your goals.

- Motivation results from information, support, and a good goal. By now, you can see that you have all three.

- Understanding how to deal with the inevitable frustrations and setbacks in life is one of the most important lessons anyone can ever learn. Remember that to get to a goal you must hang in there for the long run. Nothing worthwhile happens overnight. The best things in life take time.

*The best things in life take time.*

# Conclusion: Your Plan for Success

## Overview

This conclusion is called "Your Plan for Success" and it is really your road map for the "alternate route." Alcohol awareness has become a smaller, but still important, part of the larger goal. That goal was to learn about yourself and to become more successful and happy in your life. Congratulations on living out a big commitment to yourself, to those who care about you, and to your community. You are on your way!

Your success plan brings all of the pieces of the past few weeks together for you in powerful way. Share one key learning point you gained from each section in this workbook. What did you learn about yourself and:

1.  My Changes:

   ................................................................................................................

   ................................................................................................................

2.  My Identity:

   ................................................................................................................

   ................................................................................................................

3.  My Responsibilities:

   ................................................................................................................

   ................................................................................................................

4.  How Alcohol Got Me Here:

......................................................................................................................................

......................................................................................................................................

5.  My Relationships:

......................................................................................................................................

......................................................................................................................................

6.  My Vision:

......................................................................................................................................

......................................................................................................................................

7.  What Is Worth Reaching Toward?

......................................................................................................................................

......................................................................................................................................

8.  My Spirituality:

......................................................................................................................................

......................................................................................................................................

9.  Justice around Me:

......................................................................................................................................

......................................................................................................................................

10. My Gifts:

......................................................................................................................................

......................................................................................................................................

11. Myself and Fun:

.................................................................................................................

.................................................................................................................

12. How I'm Staying Focused:

.................................................................................................................

.................................................................................................................

Write a statement that summarizes the difference between who you were when you started this program and who you are as you finish it.

.................................................................................................................

.................................................................................................................

Who are the people who bring out the best in you? Name five of them here. Ask at least two of them to sign this plan for success as a show of support to you.

.................................................................................................................

.................................................................................................................

Name anyone who may have been harmed by your drinking behaviors. Describe what you can do to right that wrong.

.................................................................................................................

.................................................................................................................

Describe specific things you will do to stay focused on your vision and goals in the coming weeks and months.

.................................................................................................................

.................................................................................................................

.................................................................................................................

Describe specific risks that may interfere with your pursuit of your vision and goals. How will you minimize these risks?

..................................................................................................................................

..................................................................................................................................

What would you say to youth and families who are starting a program like this today?

..................................................................................................................................

..................................................................................................................................

What specific action do you plan to take to improve the lives of people in your community?

..................................................................................................................................

..................................................................................................................................

Signatures:


..........................................................          ..........................................................
Youth                                                    Diversion Worker

And in support of this youth:


..........................................................          ..........................................................
Family Member 1                                          Other Supportive Person


..........................................................          ..........................................................
Family Member 2                                          Other Supportive Person


                                                         ..........................................................
                                                         Approved by Judge

*Congratulations!*